LIFE SCIENCE

BIOMES

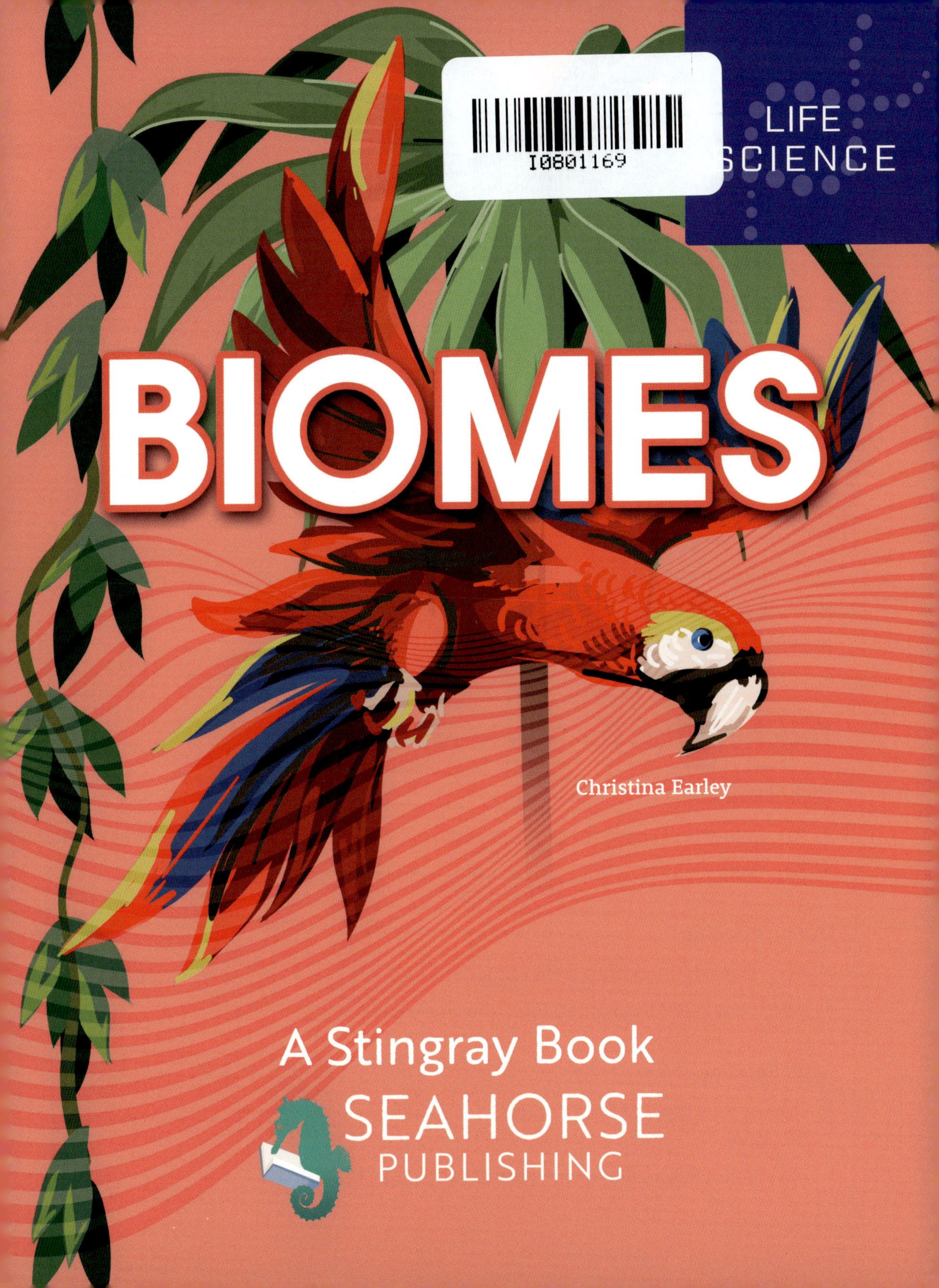

Christina Earley

A Stingray Book

SEAHORSE PUBLISHING

Teaching Tips for Caregivers and Teachers:

This Hi-Lo book features high-interest subject matter that will appeal to all readers in intermediate and middle school grades. It may be enjoyed by students reading at or above grade level as well as by those who are looking for age-appropriate themes matched with a less challenging reading level. Hi-Lo books are ideal for ELL readers, too.

Each book appeals to a striving reader's age and maturity level. Opportunities are provided for students to read words they already know while encountering a limited number of new, high-interest vocabulary words. With these supports in place, students will read more fluently while increasing reading comprehension. Use the following suggestions to help students grow as readers.

- Encourage the student to read independently at home.
- Encourage the student to practice reading aloud.
- Encourage activities that require reading.
- Establish a regular reading time.
- Have the student write questions about what they read.

Teaching Tips for Teachers:

Before Reading

- Ask, "What do I know about this topic?"
- Ask, "What do I want to learn about this topic?"

During Reading

- Ask, "What is the author trying to teach me?"
- Ask, "How is this like something I already know?"

After Reading

- Discuss how the text features (headings, index, etc.) help with understanding the topic.
- Ask, "What interesting or fun fact did you learn?"

TABLE OF CONTENTS

WHAT ARE BIOMES?

Biomes are huge areas of nature.

They have their own kind of soil and **climate**.

Each has its own plants and animals that have **adapted** to live there.

THE AQUATIC BIOME

Aquatic biomes are made of water.

Freshwater biomes, like lakes and ponds, are surrounded by land.

Marine biomes, like coral reefs and other areas of the ocean, cover 75 percent of Earth.

FUN FACTS

The largest biome on Earth is the marine biome.

THE GRASSLAND BIOME

Grassland biomes have short to tall grasses with no trees.

Just enough rain falls for grass and flowers to grow.

Bison, kangaroos, and lions live in the grassland biome.

FUN FACTS

Antarctica is the only continent without a grassland biome.

THE FOREST BIOME

Forest biomes have many trees and woody plants.

Tropical forests are hot, and some are very rainy.

Temperate forests have trees that lose their leaves.

Boreal forests are cold and snowy.

FUN FACTS

Insects that can't survive the winter will lay eggs that hatch in the spring.

THE DESERT BIOME

Only a little rain falls in a desert biome.

It can be very hot during the day and cold at night.

Plants, like the saguaro cactus, store water and use it slowly.

Coyotes, camels, and **meerkats** make their homes in the desert biome.

THE TUNDRA BIOME

The tundra biome is the coldest biome.

Ice is under the shallow soil all year.

Grass and moss are low plants that grow during the warmer summer.

Tunnels in the snow protect small **mammals** like mice in the winter.

PLANTS AND ANIMALS CHANGE ENVIRONMENTS

Animals and plants can change their **environment**.

Beavers build dams that cause flooding.

Plants that are not native can take over land.

Humans change land with buildings and farming.

FUN FACTS

People plant billions of new trees each year.

CAREER: Environmental Scientist

Environmental scientists help protect the environment.

They make plans to clean up **polluted** areas.

They take samples of air, soil, water, and food.

Some give information to people in the government who make laws.

INVESTIGATE: Make a Terrarium

Materials:

- Half-gallon or larger mason jar with lid (or similar glass jar with lid)
- Tiny river rocks or other tiny stones
- Potting soil
- Very small plants, such as succulents
- Spanish moss (optional)
- Water

Procedure:

(1) Put a layer of tiny rocks in the bottom of the jar.

(2) Pour potting soil on top of the rocks. Keep the same height as the pots your plants came in.

(3) Dig holes in the dirt large enough for the roots of your plants.

(4) Gently remove the plants from the pots and put in the holes.

(5) Add a little more dirt around the stems to keep them upright.

(6) Optional: Put Spanish moss around the plants on top of the soil.

(7) Water a very little bit. Put the lid on top.

(8) Place in an area with indirect sunlight.

THE SCIENTIFIC METHOD

- Ask a question.
- Gather information and observe.
- Make a hypothesis or guess the answer.
- Experiment and test your hypothesis, or guess.
- Analyze your test results.
- Modify your hypothesis, if necessary.
- Make a conclusion.

SCIENTIST SPOTLIGHT

Rachel Carson was a scientist and writer. Throughout her life, she wrote articles and books on sea life while working as a biologist at the U.S. Fish and Wildlife Service. Her book *Silent Spring* convinced people of the importance of taking care of the environment. It explained the effect of pesticides on the food chain. Rachel Carson is known as the mother of the environmentalist movement.

GLOSSARY

adapted (uh-DAP-tid): changed to survive

biomes (BYE-ohmz): areas of the world with similar climates, animals, and plants

bison (BYE-suhn): very large mammals with large heads, humped shoulders, and short horns that are curved

climate (KLYE-mit): the usual weather conditions in an area over a long period of time

environment (en-VYE-ruhn-muhnt): everything that surrounds a certain type of living thing

freshwater (FRESH-waw-tur): having to do with water that is not salty

mammals (MAM-uhlz): warm-blooded animals with fur or hair and skeletons inside their bodies

marine (muh-REEN): having to do with the sea or ocean

meerkats (MEER-katz): small mammals with broad heads, large eyes, pointed snouts, long legs, and thin tapering tails

polluted (puh-LOO-tid): made dirty or harmful to health by adding waste material

INDEX

AFTER READING QUESTIONS

1. What are two types of aquatic biomes?
2. Describe the tundra biome.
3. How do people change the environment?

About the Author

Christina Earley lives in South Florida with her husband, son, and dog. Her favorite subject in school was science. She enjoys learning the science behind the world around her, such as how roller coasters work. She loves mint chocolate chip ice cream and mermaids.

Written by: Christina Earley
Design by: Kathy Walsh
Editor: Kim Thompson

Library of Congress PCN Data
Biomes / Christina Earley
Life Science
ISBN 978-1-63897-493-2 (hard cover)
ISBN 978-1-63897-608-0 (paperback)
ISBN 978-1-63897-723-0 (EPUB)
ISBN 978-1-63897-838-1 (eBook)
Library of Congress Control Number: 2022930845

Printed in the United States of America.

Photographs/Shutterstock: Cover & Title pg © Yumeee, ©Vlad RA27, ©N1chEZ: Pg 3-23 ©N1chEZ; Pg 7, 9, 11, 17 ©Olga_C; Pg 5 ©manfredstutz, © Tory Kallman, ©Martin Pelanek; Pg 6-7 ©Vlad61; Pg 6 ©Irina Wilhauk; Pg 8-9 ©Pav-Pro Photography Ltd; Pg 8 ©Ghost Bear; Pg 9 ©vladsilver; Pg 10 ©Brina L. Bunt; Pg 11 ©Silmiart; Pg 12 ©LHBLLC, ©Martin Mecnarowski; Pg 14 © Incredible Arctic; Pg 15 ©Risto Puranen, ©FotoRequest; Pg 16 ©Chase Dekker; Pg 17 ©Valentin Valkov, ©J.K. York; ©Maksim Safaniuk; Pg 18 ©Marcin Balcerzak; Pg 19 ©Chayanin Wongpracha; Pg 21 ©Marusya Chaika, ©Pixel-Shot

Seahorse Publishing Company
www.seahorsepub.com

Published in the United States
Seahorse Publishing
PO Box 771325
Coral Springs, FL 33077

SEAHORSE PUBLISHING